Memories of Easley South Carolina

My Wonderful Grandparents
Leigh and Camella Hendricks Hunt
And Their Descendants

By Granddaughter Judith Willis White
2020

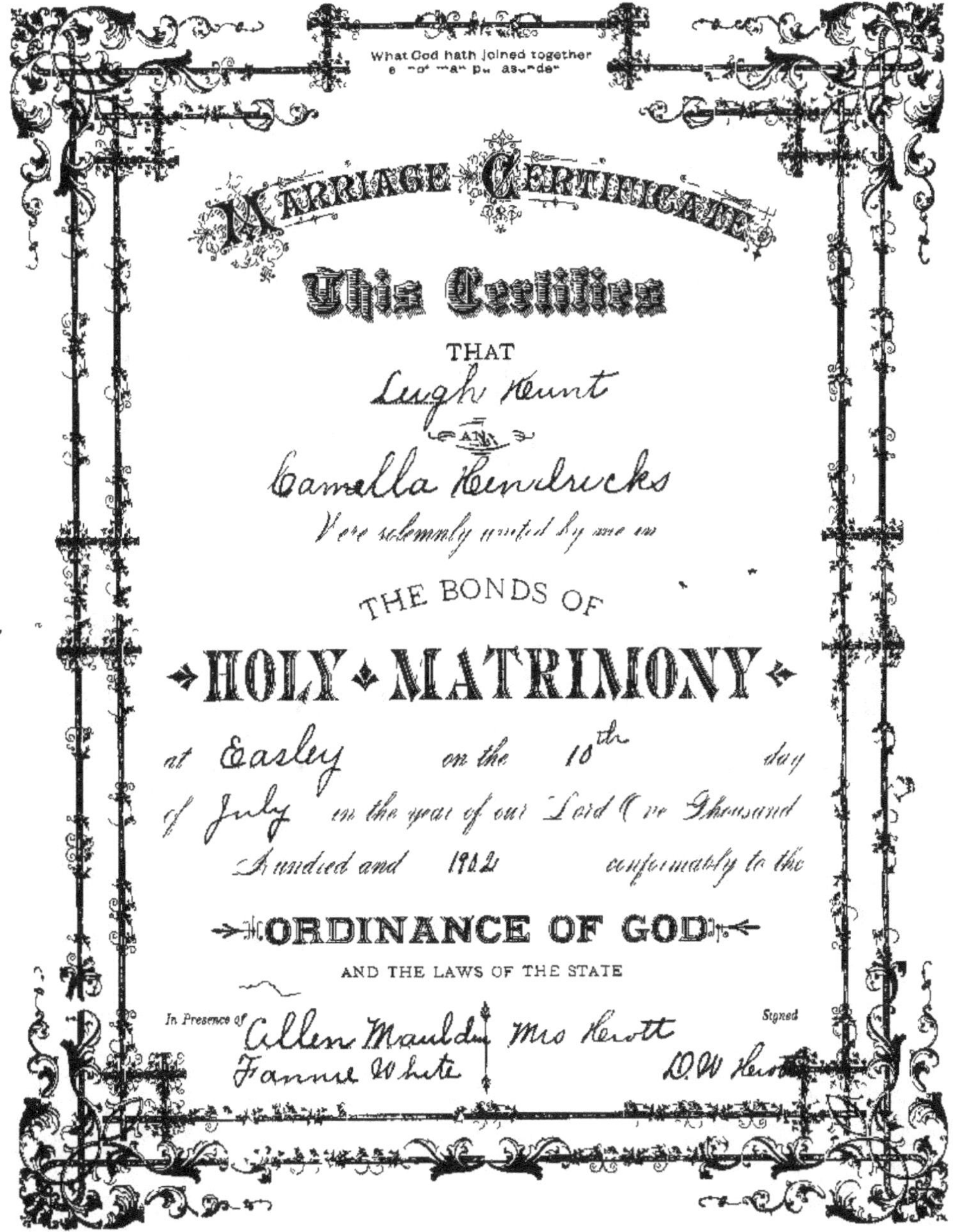
What God hath joined together
let not man put asunder

MARRIAGE CERTIFICATE

This Certifies

THAT

Leigh Hunt

AND

Camella Hendricks

Were solemnly united by me in

THE BONDS OF

HOLY MATRIMONY

at Easley on the 10th day
of July in the year of our Lord One Thousand
Hundred and 1912 conformably to the

ORDINANCE OF GOD

AND THE LAWS OF THE STATE

In Presence of Allen Mauldin Mrs Hewott
Fannie White

Signed
D. W. Hewott

Dedication

To my husband Howard, who patiently spent many hours formatting, inserting pictures and helping me finish this project!

Also, to my cousins and family, whose relationship I cherish. I hope we have many more fun-filled times together.

Memories of

Easley

South Carolina

My Wonderful Grandparents,
Leigh and Camella Hendricks Hunt
And their Descendants

By Judith Willis White

2020

Table of Contents

Chapter 1: Cora Camella Hendricks (1882-1954)

Wow, a lot has happened since we gathered in Easley on July 10th, 2002, to celebrate and commemorate the 100th anniversary of our grandparents wedding. Like all families, we have experienced happiness grief, weddings, births, quarantining from corona virus and sadly, deaths since we were together in 2002.

Cora Camella Hendricks (1882-1954)

Leigh Hunt (April 30, 1868-February 2, 1960) and Camella Hendricks (September 24, 1882-April 23, 1954) met when Leigh was boarding near the Hendricks' home and working nearby. That was about the year 1900. William McKinley, who would be assassinated the next year, was President of the United States. Ford Motor Company was established and, two years later, the Wright Brothers would make their historic flight at Kitty Hawk, North Carolina. It would be twenty years before women would receive the right to vote in 1920.

Camella Hendricks at age 19

18-year-old Cora Camella Hendricks went by her long-time nickname, "Mella." She must have been pretty smitten by this tall, handsome 32-year-old man as she broke off her serious relationship with Rufe Ashmore, her boyfriend at the time. When Mella met Leigh, he was working at a place that one his daughters later called "the government distillery" near Pickens. The job was near the Hendricks' farm, and he boarded nearby. They met and fell in love. You see, in addition to his day-job, Leigh played fiddle at barn dances all around the area. His musical talent may have been an attraction, for Mella loved music.

Two years later, on July 10th, 1902, they were married at the home of a friend, by Reverend D. W. Heiott, the pastor of Griffin Baptist Church, even though her parents very much disapproved—probably because of the 14 year age difference (he was 34 and she was 19). The parents did not attend. Those in attendance were Allen Mauldin,

Mrs. Heiott, Fannie White and DW Heiott.

Recently, having been involved with writing our own personal memoirs, I realized how much those early visits to Leigh and Camella's home had meant to me, even though I was only 13 when my grandmother died and their home was sold. She made each one of her many grandchildren feel so special, and I was totally convinced I was her favorite -- at least until my cousin Edward Galyon was born in 1947.

Mella looked the part of the perfect grandmother, one that Norman Rockwell might paint because she was short, rather plump with her white hair pulled into a bun on the back of her head, which made her look much older. She always wore ankle length dresses and smelled of "Evening in Paris" perfume. She loved to laugh, sing, cook, rock on the porch and gather up grandchildren onto her ample lap.

Cora Camella Hendricks was the seventh of twelve children born to David Ervin Hendricks (1847-1908) and Vashti Elizabeth Anthony (1848-1933). She was named for her mother's sister, Dorcas Camella (or Camelia) Jane, who was born in 1854. Mella was born on September 24, 1882, and raised in the Griffin section of Pickens County, South Carolina.

On September 23, 1864, her father David Ervin Hendricks, who was 16 years old, enlisted into South Carolina troops for defense of his state in the Civil War. He was called up in October, but when he was at Mt. Pleasant military camp, near Charleston, South Carolina, he contracted measles, was discharged on April 9, 1865 and sent home to recover. This discharge probably saved his life. David lost two brothers in the Civil War: John Baylus and William Fields. John Baylus lost an arm in a battle near Chancellorsville, Virginia, got gangrene and died in a

Home of David Ervin and Betty Hendricks in Dacusville, South Carolina

Virginia hospital. William Fields lost his life in a battle, also near Chancellorsville.

So David Ervin was the only surviving male heir and as a result, he inherited a large tract of land in the Dacusville area of Pickens County from his parents George (1802-1881) and Louvicy (1812-1892) Hendricks on which he built his house. This land included three small mountains. The Hendricks home was the first in the area to have running water, which was supplied by a long wooden trough that came down from distant Glassy Mountain. David was on the Board of Directors of the Pickens Cotton Mill and a large holder of preferred stock, which would pay handsome dividends for many years. He was a successful farmer as well. He also owned and operated a roller mill, a post office and a store. Furthermore, David was the organist at Griffin Baptist Church.   A strong work ethic was instilled in each of the twelve children. Each child was expected to participate in the farm chores during the summer months. Nine of the twelve children attended college, which was very unusual for the time.

Glassy Mountain behind the Hendricks' farm

Griffin Baptist Church was an integral part of their family life. Mella's great-grandfather, Sargeant Griffin (1778-1858), gave the land for the church and made a large contribution in 1857, "seeing the good that might arise from a Baptist church in the neighborhood." The church was named for him, and the original document is still displayed in the church today in his handwriting. Many of Sargeant and Averilla Griffin's descendants attend church there today, and many of our ancestors are buried in the cemetery.

Mella and her sisters attended Glassy Mountain School, which was next door to their house, about 200 yards away. The house has been torn down and all that remains today is the over-grown Glassy Mountain Cemetery, which was next to the school. David Ervin's parents, George and Louvicy, are buried there, side by side. Strangely enough, George's stone reads "George Hendrix" and her stone reads "Louvicy Mulinox, wife of George Hendricks." Note that the spelling of the last names differs. George Hendrix had burned to death while clearing new ground in 1881 and his stone has this long inscription on it: "He lived a Christian life, but sad to the memory of his many friends, companions and children, he was burned to death July 6, 1881. But, dear friends, do not weep for me, but remember while you are standing around my grave, thinking of the awful condition of my body, that my soul is blooming anew in Heaven."

Chapter 2: Leigh Hunt (1868-1960)

Like Mella, Leigh Hunt was a seventh child. His parents were William Uriah Hunt (1830-1894) and Martha Jane Blythe (1831-1892). He was named for the poet Leigh Hunt, who was not related, but whose poetry his mother loved. Leigh was born on April 30, 1868, and was raised in the

Leigh Hunt in his 30's.

From left to right; back row, Edna, Frances and Wesley; front row, Grace, Sara Bess and Ruth.

Dacusville area of Pickens County, South Carolina. William Uriah Hunt, Leigh's father, was a surveyor, farmer, and an officer in the Civil War who was taken prisoner, sent to Johnson Island on Lake Erie and almost starved to death, surviving by eating rats. The war and imprisonment took a toll on William and his family, both physically and emotionally. There were nine children in the family and Leigh was the second child born after his father returned from the war. Martha Jane, Leigh's mother, loved to read, and one of her daughters, Dora (1855-1914) moved to Texas and became a well-known author and literary critic, writing under the pen name, "The Far East." William and Martha had a large farm with many acres at Dacusville. On his father's deathbed, Leigh promised that he would care for his unmarried sisters after he inherited the farm. This would cause friction in the family years later. For example, one of Leigh's sisters, Rebecca (1857-1944), who was always referred to as "Old Aunt Becky," proved to be a challenge for everyone. Mella did not look forward to the occasional episodes when Becky would come over to live with them for several weeks while a spat with her husband, Mr. Groce, cooled off. While she was visiting, she would give the Hunt children piano lessons, which, apparently, wasn't particularly enjoyable. One time when "Old Aunt Becky" was leaving, she said to Leigh, "You've got some fine children except for that Grace. She's going to give you trouble." Unfortunately, Grace was hiding behind the door and overheard this.

Leigh and Mella's first home in Dacusville, South Carolina

Chapter 3: Mr. and Mrs. Leigh Hunt

Leigh's parents had died several years before he and Mella married in 1902, five years before Oklahoma became a state. The newlyweds lived in the Hunt family log house in Dacusville, South Carolina. Leigh soon constructed a large two-story house across the road. This would be their home for 17 years and where 6 of their seven children would be born.

New House in Easley, South Carolina

In 1919, Leigh and Mella moved their large family from Dacusville to Easley, South Carolina. Frances was 15 years old and Edna was 13. The couple wanted the children to benefit from the better schools "in town", and the Glassy Mountain School had closed. Leigh purchased a Sears, Roebuck and

Leigh and Mella's new house in Easley, South Carolina

Edna, Frances and Wesley

Company two-story kit house, which was delivered by railroad as lumber, etc. It was partially paid for with the handsome dividends from David Hendrick's (Mella's father) preferred stock in the Pickens Cotton Mill. It was constructed on a lot at 301 South 1st Street in front of an existing barn. At that time the street was not much more than a dirt path running down to a swamp that later became Easley High School. The house and barn are still standing today. Leigh would later add a large vegetable and flower garden, chicken houses, orchard, and animal pens. Their new house had, on the first floor, a wrap-around front and side porch, parlor, large dining room, basic kitchen, back screened "sleeping" porch, and three bedrooms. Upstairs, there were four large bedrooms and one bath. The large house was heated by coal stoves in each room. By the front door sat the

Leigh and Mella's new 1920 Studebaker.

hand-cranked Edison record player, which I now own. Long ago, it would entertain the grandchildren for hours, playing the thick records, most of which had been selected by Mella.

About the same time, Leigh and Mella purchased their first car, a 1920 Studebaker. On the day of delivery, while Leigh and Mella were reading the operator's manual in the house, 14-year-old Edna, loaded her brothers and sisters in the car and drove around Easley. Needless to say, her father was very upset.

Leigh and Mella lived in Easley in this beautiful home for 35 years. They had seven children who lived to adulthood: four girls and three boys. Leigh ran his store in downtown Easley while Mella stayed home with their large family. Bruce and a stillborn daughter would be born in Easley. The siblings remained very close throughout their lives, always gathering in Easley every summer. As a result, my cousins and I have also remained close.

In later years, local "old maid schoolteachers" rented two of the upstairs bedrooms, which gave Leigh and Camella additional income. Teachers Miss Eva VanLandingham, her sister Miss Alma VanLandingham, and Miss Helen Mozingo lived there for

Mella and Leigh and some of their many grandchildren in 1946

years. The house was filled with wonderful smells of fried chicken and pound cake, laughter and fun. As a young girl I had absolutely no idea or appreciation of the work and planning that went into the family gatherings!

Mella's Missionary Society, First Baptist Church, Easley

Cousins: Judith, Susanne, Jim and Will

I remember that, when my aunts, uncles and cousins came to Easley for family gatherings, my girl cousins and I would fight over who would get to sleep with Mella, and, as I remember, the limit was four. The double bed would "jiggle" with her laughter after we would all pile in and curl up to her ample body. Then we would start questioning her on subjects we would not dare ask our mothers. During the day, raising her voice or scolding us never happened, even when we would run around on the roof, peaking in windows, spying on the teachers. I cringe when I think about how we'd sit in the old barn loft, surrounded by hay and smoking the cigarettes we'd sneaked from our mothers' packs of Marlboros. Evenings were filled with playing "blind-man's bluff" in the front yard, or gathering around the old, out-of-tune upright piano in the front parlor with my cousins. My sister Suzanne would play it with Mella singing her off-pitch version of "Bringing in the Sheets" -- at the top of her lungs -- followed by bursts of laughter from all of us. Hard to imagine how much fun we had without computers, internet or cell phones!

Mella was always active in the First Baptist Church and the Missionary Society, doing kind deeds for anyone in need. She was adored by all who had the privilege of knowing her. Mella always felt that Leigh would predecease her since he was 14 years older but ironically, he would out-live her by 6 years.

Leigh owned and operated Leigh Hunt's Hay Grain and Provisions in Easley, and did a little farming on the side. He was soft spoken, very tall (six feet) thin and always dressed in a suit and tie. Leigh was a deacon at the First Baptist Church for many years. He loved to carefully "roll his own" cigarettes between his long, tobacco-stained fingers, always keeping the much needed supplies in his pocket. He would take a few puffs, knock the burning end off and put the remainder in his pocket. More than once, Leigh would have smoke coming out of his pocket from the smoldering cigarette, but fortunately never suffered any bodily harm. He kept a bottle of blackberry wine hidden in the sleeping porch for an occasional nip, hoping it would not be discovered by disapproving Mella. He could often be found curled up on the daybed,

Leigh and Mella at their 50th Wedding Anniversary, July 10, 1952

Westview Cemetery, Easley, South Carolina

located in the corner of the dining room taking a nap while noisy grandchildren played nearby. We loved it when he'd take out his fiddle and play "Arkansas Traveler" for all of us, something he would even do at his 90th birthday party at my home in Nashville, Tennessee. His fiddle, which Leigh purchased from a peddler who claimed it was a "genuine Stradivarius," is still in the family. It is owned by Suzanne Willis Potter's daughter, Claire Gonzalez (Leigh's great-granddaughter) who still plays it today.

Mella and Leigh Buried in Easley

On April 23, 1954, two months before the marriage of her first granddaughter, my sister, Suzanne Willis, and seven months before the birth of her last granddaughter, Martha Galyon, Mella suffered a sudden and massive coronary heart attack and died at age 72. She had a history of uncontrolled high blood pressure. At her funeral, the First Baptist Church in Easley was filled with flowers, family and friends mourning her death. She is buried on a large Hunt Family plot in Westview Cemetery in Easley. She had selected this large burial plot in hopes that some of their family members would be buried there. At this time the ones buried there are Mella and Leigh, Frances and Henry Watkins, EB (Nookie) Hunt, Linda Harlan, and Chris Harlan.

After Mella's death, Leigh lived with his children, moving about to not overly burden any one family. He died almost six years later, on February 2, 1960, at the age of 90 years. He is buried beside Mella in Westview Cemetery.

Breaking up the Easley Household

A few months after Mella's death, the decision was made to sell the Easley house, and distribute most of the furnishings among the Hunt heirs. But, some furnishings remained with the house, including the beautiful oak, claw-footed dining table, on which all of the family meals had been served. Aunt Francis remembered Leigh and Mella, hooking up the horse and buggy and going to Greenville to buy furniture from a professor who was selling everything, including this table, in order to move out West. In 1955, Ansel Jameson and his wife bought the house and barn from the estate for $10,000, and they lived there for about forty years. In 1995, Ansel bequeathed the dining table to me in his will. Howard and I quickly moved it to our home in Charlotte, where it remains, is loved and used daily. John and Christine Sitton of Easley purchase the house after Mr. Jameson's death. In recent years others have owned the house, which was renovated, and for a time was operated as a Bed and Breakfast. Most recently, it has been further renovated by a young couple who are so excited about raising their children there. The old barn still stands.

Chapter 4: The 100th Wedding Anniversary Gathering of Hunt Descendants

Realizing that the 100th anniversary of our grandparents' wedding was coming up, I decided to put together a little booklet about the Hunt family. With my husband Howard's help, I proceeded to compose a booklet and to plan a Hunt family reunion in Easley, South Carolina. After a few days of gathering names, dates and stories, we finished our little epistle. With invitations issued, we traveled to Easley to make all of the final arrangements. We were so pleased and excited at the response – 30-plus family members would be coming. On a hot, Saturday afternoon on July 10th, 2002, we all checked into the Comfort Inn in Easley. After affectionate hugs, greetings and compliments, we had fun catching up on family news while hanging out by the pool.

The 100th Anniversary gathering in Easley, South Carolina on July 10, 2002 to commemorate the marriage of Leigh and Mella Hunt

Later, trying to look our best, we proceeded to the Smithfield Country Club for a dinner. My talented sister and her husband Tom entertained us after dinner with some lively music, followed by many of the cousins sharing funny stories from our childhood visits to Leigh and Mella's. One of my favorites was our Great Falls cousin, Laurens Fort's hilarious description, delivered with his South Carolina drawl, on how Leigh had to always put one hand on his face to keep his head from drifting to one side – the result of nerve damage to his neck from an earlier automobile accident. Laurens told how, as a little boy, he would sit on Leigh's lap in the car when it was raining, operating the manual windshield wipers, while Leigh had one hand on the steering wheel and the other held his head straight.

After an early breakfast on Sunday morning, we lined up a convoy of cars and headed down some dusty roads to see old home places and cemeteries. We saw Leigh and Mella's first home in Dacusville, which had been built on Leigh's parent's farm soon after their marriage in 1902. Then we saw Mella's parents, Betty and Ervin Hendrick's home and the family cemetery right next to the house. We also visited Griffin Baptist Church. We visited the home of Mella's grandparents, George and Louvicy Hendricks, where we saw the burns in the floor from when General Sherman's Yankees tried to burn the house down. We went to the Hunt Cemetery where Leigh's parents, William Uriah and Martha Jane Hunt, and his grandparents, Martin and Martha Hunt, are buried, and had lunch with a distant Hunt cousin who lived nearby. It was a very memorable weekend of learning, laughing and sharing the love of our family!

Chapter 5: Children and Descendants of Mella and Leigh Hunt -- Baby Helen

Leigh and Mella's first little baby, Helen (April 27, 1903—May 14, 1903) was born with a throat defect that prevented her from swallowing. She lived only 23 days. Their grief brought about reconciliation with Mella's parents. They buried their little baby girl at Griffin Baptist Church.

Chapter 5: Children and Descendants of Mella and Leigh Hunt -- Frances

Frances (October 26, 1904--January 8, 2000), and her sister Edna, who was 18 months younger, would attend school together through college. They both graduated from Winthrop College in Rock Hill, South Carolina, in 1926, when Winthrop was still a women's college. It was during this time that the 19th amendment was passed (August 1920) giving women the right to vote.

Frances was always thin, and her hair turned white hair prematurely. On June 20, 1934, she married Joseph Henry Watkins, Ph. D. (March 18, 1900 - September 8, 1964) a close friend of Larry Willis, Edna's husband. Larry and Edna actually introduced them. Henry received his

Francis Hunt

doctorate from the University of North Carolina. Dr. Watkins taught at The Citadel and was a recognized Professor of Chemistry and Geology. They lived in faculty housing on the campus in Charleston throughout their married life. Frances taught second grade at Ashley Hall School in Charleston for more than 25 years. After Henry's unexpected death in 1964, Frances moved to a little house on "The Battery" in downtown Charleston. Howard and I

Francis and Henry Watkins, about 1932

always loved to visit her when we'd go down for the Spoleto Festival every year. Her home was so warm and welcoming and her meals were served so elegantly always with beautiful table linens, silver and china. When warm weather would arrive in the spring, Frances would have all of her beautiful oriental rugs removed and white slipcovers placed on all of the furniture. This was her "Rite of Spring."

Frances was so proud of her family heritage and was a member of the Daughters of the American Revolution (DAR). She went into the DAR on our Revolutionary War relative, Robert Bowen (1740-1817).

In 1989, Frances moved to Durham, North Carolina, to be near her daughter Linda and her grandchildren. She and Henry are buried at Westview Cemetery in Easley in the Hunt family plot. Because she was the oldest child, Frances was very responsible, and this nurturing trait continued throughout her life.

Children of Frances and Henry Watkins

Frances and Henry had one daughter, Linda.

1.   Linda Harlan (November 27, 1937 - November 6, 2002) was married to Dr. William Robert Harland, Jr. (November 1, 1930), and later to Martin Carmichael (1927 - August 10, 2005). Linda and Bill had two children.

a. Dr. Elizabeth Anthony Harlan (July 27, 1960) married Dr. James Earl Crowe, Jr. (August 14, 1961). They have two children:

1. Stephen Elliott Crowe (December 18, 1990) married Ericka Joanne Sanchez (July 1, 1990).
2. Catherine Grace Crowe (August 10, 1993).

b. Dr. William Robert Harlan, III (May 10, 1962) married Betsy Stelzenmuller (December 31, 1962). They have three children:

1. Elizabeth Brennan Harlan (October 31, 1993) married Jonathan Lovejoy (May 16, 1986)
2. Mary Chamberlain Harlan (July 11, 1997).
3. William Robert Harlan, IV (January 9, 2000).

c. Christopher Hunt Harlan (February 17, 1973 - November 22, 2008).

Chapter 6: Children and Descendants of Mella and Leigh Hunt -- Edna

Edna Leigh (March 6, 1906 - May 10, 1981) was eighteen months younger than her sister Frances. The sisters were close as children and would remain close, always attending school together. The story has been told that, when attending Mount Carmel Elementary School, they would ride their horse Dixie three to four miles to Dr. Milton Ponder's house, which was directly across the street from the school. Dr. Ponder was a cousin and delivered eight of the Hunt babies.

Edna Hunt

Edna and Larry Willis

Edna received a B.S. degree from Winthrop College at age 20, majoring in biology and graduating with honors. She and Aunt Frances were roommates and both graduated from Winthrop in 1926. Edna skipped her senior year in high school in order that she and Frances would go to Winthrop together and be in the same graduating class. Their Uncle Absalom Blythe, who was a prominent attorney in Greenville, paid for some of their college tuition. After graduation, Edna taught school for 4 years in Easley before pursuing a master degree at the University of South Carolina in Columbia, where she met Larry Jordan Willis from Travelers Rest,

SC. They married on June 4, 1930, in Easley, in the parlor of her parents' home.

Larry's first job was teaching at the Citadel in Charleston. Before long, the couple moved to Tryon, North Carolina, where Larry was superintendent of schools. In 1937 Edna and Larry then moved to Nashville, Tennessee, with their 3-year-old daughter Suzanne, to permit Larry to complete his Doctorate at Peabody College. Edna typed dissertations, took in wash and worked at the war office downtown to help support the family during this time. (By the way, Howard recently published Larry's Ph. D. dissertation as a book, *Advancing American Reading Achievement During the Great Depression*, which is available on Amazon.com). Larry completed his doctorate degree in 1938 and became a high school principle in Nashville Public Schools and soon after became Supervisor of Nashville Elementary Schools.

I was born on May 21, 1941. Over a year and a half before my birth, World War II fighting had been going on in Europe as Hitler's Nazi's fought their military campaign to conquer much of Europe while also eliminating Europe's Jewish people. Seven months after my birth Japanese Imperialists would attack America's Hawaiian Islands territory at Pearl Harbor, the first strike in Imperial Japan's military campaign to conquer the western Pacific countries. America would enter both wars, the European War and the Pacific War, immediately after the attack on our navy warships at Pearl Harbor. This was the time America's "Greatest Generation" rose up

and, together, by amazing efforts at home and abroad, saved the world for freedom and democracy.

About the same time Larry was diagnosed with and had surgery for a brain tumor. It was a very difficult time for them with Larry's recovery, a new baby, a seven year old daughter and very little money! My mother was always so appreciative of her brother Wesley for paying part of Larry's hospital bills. His brain tumor would return 4 years later in 1945. It was truly a miracle that he survived not one, but 2 brain surgeries in the 40s. Although it left him with a noticeable limp, Larry had a very successful career in the Nashville City Schools. Edna was always a South Carolinian at heart, and hoped someday to return to the place of her birth but they never left Nashville.

Edna had a strong drive and a competitive spirit but was sensitive to a fault. Although, she was not a musician herself, she wanted my sister and me to play the piano and an instrument, for which I am so grateful! We have both had a lifetime of enjoyment and fulfillment from our music. My sister still plays her violin and I still play the French horn.

When I was growing up there were 2 things we never missed-church and symphony concerts, no matter how sick or tired we were! Later my sister and I both played in the Nashville symphony.

Edna died on Mother's Day, May 10, 1981, three months before my son David was born, after a long-fought battle with cancer. Larry died three years later, on July 27, 1984 also of cancer. They were married for 51 years. Both are buried at Woodlawn Cemetery in Nashville Tennessee.

The Daughters of Edna and Larry Willis

Edna and Larry had two daughters:

1.   Suzanne Willis, (September 23, 1934) married Dr. William Paxton Parker (February 11, 1930—May 6, 2005), with whom she had two sons. Then she married Raymond Paul Poggenburg, Jr., Ph. D. (May 28, 1926 - March 14, 2004), with whom she had a daughter. Then she married Thomas Potter, Ph. D. (July 1, 1941).

a.   William Paxton Parker, III (August 15, 1955) married Claire Cawood (June 9, 1963). They have 3 children:

1. Mary Catherine Parker (July 24, 1995).

2. Virginia Claire Parker (December 29, 1996).

3. William Paxton Parker, IV (September 16, 1999).

b.   David Laurence Parker (December 31, 1959) married Olga Biescas (September 16, 1961) on December 30, 1988. They have 2 children:

1.   Camille Mercedes Parker (October29, 1992).

2.   Emma Jordan Parker (December 23, 1995).

c.   Claire Poggenburg (October 22, 1970) married Jose Delfin Gonzalez (June 1, 1968). They have 2 children:

i.   Jose Eduardo Gonzalez (Oct 15, 1998).

ii.   Ana Claire Gonzalez (November 20, 2000).

2.   Judith Hunt Willis (May 21, 1941) married Howard Ray White, Jr. (August 4, 1938) on August 24, 1959. They have three children, two of which are living.

a.   Howard Ray White, III (February 21, 1962-- October 31, 1981).

b.   Keith Jordan White (February 19, 1964) married Dr. Kelley Elizabeth Morris (September 23, 1965) on August 2, 1986.

i.   Dr. Alexandria Jordan White (July 20th, 1993).

ii.   Stephen Michael White (June 10th, 1996).

c.   David Howard White (September 4, 1981) married Christine Ozwarzak (June 21, 1985) on May 3, 2008.

Chapter 8: Children and Descendants of Mella and Leigh Hunt -- James Wesley

Wesley Hunt

James Wesley Hunt (May 1, 1907—May 22, 1987) was educated in the Easley schools and received a B. S. degree in Business Administration from the University of South Carolina. He graduated cum laude and received the Delta Sigma Pi Scholarship key, awarded to the most outstanding student in Business Administration. He formed his own company, J. W. Hunt Company, an accounting

Wesley, Marie Hunt and their children

firm with many offices in South Carolina.

He married Emma Marie Edwards (May 27, 1908—June 10, 1998) of Columbia, South Carolina. She was an accomplished ballet dancer, but later developed arthritis, most likely caused by Lyme disease from a tick bite She was confined to a wheelchair for the rest of her life. Both Wesley and Marie are buried in Elmwood Cemetery in Columbia. Wesley was a successful and respected businessman. They lived most of their married life at 2424 Duncan Street, Columbia, S. C.

They had six children.

    1.   James Wesley Hunt, Jr. (June 27, 1934) married Jo-Ann Loadholt (January 1, 1940) on July 15, 1961. They had one child:

a. James Wesley Hunt, III (August 15, 1963 - November 13, 2005).

    i. James Wesley Hunt, IV (July 14, 1996)

    ii. Macie Hunt (September 25, 1998)

2. William Rion Hunt (June 4, 1936) married Selina MacNulty (March 10, 1941—March 6, 2003) on February 22, 1958, then married Emmala Barnett (January 4, 1935). Will and Selena had 2 children:

a. William Rion Hunt, Jr (October 15, 1960).

    i. Robert Collins Hunt (April 4, 1991)
    ii. William Wesley Hunt (May 25, 1995)

b. Dr. Selina Roberdeau Hunt (June 9, 1964) married Dr. Scott Douglas Augustine on July 7, 1984, then married William Russell McKinney, Jr on June 1, 2006. Selina and Scott have 3 children:

    i. Selina Brielle Hunt-Augustine (February 1985)
    ii. Jonathan Scott-Augustine (August 1990)
    iii. William Blakely–Augustine (August 1993)

3. Edward Leigh Hunt (June 14, 1938) married Adorée Leon (September 17, 1937) on October 22, 1961. They have 2 children:

a. Heidi Adorée Hunt (June 22, 1962) married Frank Gerard Sherlock (July 27, 1960), the father of their two daughters and later married Robert Andrew Billek (June 17, 1953).

    i. Britleigh Kayla Sherlock (September 8, 1990).

    ii. Brielle Adoree Sherlock (October 20, 1992)

b. Edward Leigh Hunt, Jr. (November 3, 1963).

4. Dr. Robert Bridger Hunt (January 23, 1940 - December 2, 2004) married Katherine Edith Lane (August 11, 1945) on April 25, 1970.

a. James Devereaux Hunt (May, 30, 1971) married Alexandra Elaine Crawford.

i. Robert Bridger Hunt II (August 20, 2004)
ii. James Dereveraux Hunt (September 23, 2005)

5. Marie Edwards Hunt (December 13, 1943) married Wycliffe Eskrigge Haynes (April 29. 1943) on August 20, 1965. They had one child:

a. Ivan Wycliffe Haynes (February 20, 1971 - January 10, 2018).

6. Dr. Jettie Vivian Hunt (June 15, 1950) married Dr. Michael J. Lotz (February 4, 1938 – June 19, 2019)

Chapter 9: Children and Descendants of Mella and Leigh Hunt -- Grace

Grace Hunt (August 22, 1909—December 4, 1997) also attended Winthrop College, and graduated in 1930. She taught Home Economics in Great Falls High School, where she met her future husband, Dr. Laurens Warren Fort (April 4, 1894—March 14, 1976). They married on May 25, 1935 and lived in Great Falls all of their married life, where Dr. Fort had a dental practice until he turned the practice over to his son, also a dentist. Over the years, Grace and Dr. Fort also accumulated several farms in the county and many rental houses in and around Great Falls. Grace was enthusiastic and energetic, the third of four sisters. She liked to mention that she could play the piano, drive a car and dance by the time she was twelve years old. No matter how many family members were at the Fort's house for a meal, she and a long-time maid, Ella Mae, made everyone feel welcome. Ella Mae's Southern fried chicken was

Grace Hunt

amazing! Grace was devoted to her church, played the organ and sang in the choir for over 50 years at Mt. Dearborn Methodist Church in Great Falls. Both Grace and Dr. Fort are buried at Greenlawn Cemetery in Great Falls.

Children of Grace and Dr. Fort

Grace and Dr. Fort had two children.

1. Sara Jefferies Fort (July 21, 1936-July 16 2018) married Col. Charles Hicklen Ferguson (December 4, 1933--August 15, 2017). Sara and Charlie had 5 children:

a. Carolyn Grace Ferguson (December 28, 1956) married William

Dudley Fowler, Sr. (August 21, 1984). Carolyn and William have 2 children:

    i. William Dudley Fowler, Jr. (August 21, 1984) married Kathryn Powell (November 6, 1985). William and Kathryn have 3 children:

        a. William Dudley Fowler, III (June 14, 2013)

        b. Wenn Powell Fowler (February 19, 2015).

        c. Virginia Grace Fowler (September 28, 2016).

    ii. Laura Elizabeth Fowler (September 22, 1987) married Marcus Taylor McKnight (February 17, 1988). Laura and Marcus have one child:

        a. Caroline Grace McKnight (March 10, 2018).

b. Charles Hicklen Ferguson, Jr. (January 13, 1960) married Loreta Jones (September 21, 1958). Charles and Loreta have one daughter:

    i. Amy Elise Ferguson (March 25, 1991) married Justin Philip Bernardo (June 9, 1993).

c. Jack Lyle Ferguson (July 12, 1961--August 24, 2008) married Mary Krucher (June 12, 1959). They had 2 children:

    i. Jack Lyle Ferguson, Jr. (December 3, 1982).

    ii. Patrick James Ferguson (September 18, 1984) married Stephanie Grable (September 19, 1986). Patrick and Stephanie have four children:

        a. Aidyn Lucas Ferguson (February 6, 2007).

        b. Wendy Jo Ferguson (August 5, 2009).

        c. Charles Anthony Ferguson (March 28, 2012).

        d. Catherine Grace Ferguson (July 7, 2014).

d. Laura Fort Ferguson (July 7, 1961) married Edgar Madison Jolley,

Jr. (July 7, 1961). Laura and Edgar have 4 children:

    i.   Carolyn Grace Jolley (January 15, 1988) married Kevin Christopher Stephens (January 25, 1985). Carolyn and Kevin have one child:

        a.   Owen Andrew Stephens (May 6, 2018).

    ii. Edgar Madison Jolley, III (June 1, 1989).

    iii. Zackary Collins Jolley (December 28, 1992) married Page Roberts (January 31, 1991).

    iv. Sara Catherine Jolley (April 22, 1994--February 2, 2011).

  e.   Sam Jefferies Ferguson (October 10, 1964).

2.   Dr. Laurens Warren Fort, Jr. (March 18, 1940 - March 23, 2017) married Brenda Seebold (June 24, 1945). Laurens and Brenda had two children:

  a.   Laurens Warren Fort, III (August 1, 1968).

  b.   James Shannon Fort (April 13, 1971). James has 4 children:

    i.   Christian Blaine Banks (March 12, 1997).

    ii. Matthew Kendrick Fort (October 19, 1998).

    iii. Justin Case Fort (October 16, 2007).

    iv. Jesse James Fort (November 13, 2008).

Chapter 10: Children and Descendants of Mella and Leigh Hunt -- Little Ruth

Ruth Hunt (November 3, 1911—June 16, 1916) contracted spinal meningitis when she was almost six years old. On the Friday she was dying, Leigh went upstairs, woke up the children, and said, "wake up, our little darling is dying." All the children went downstairs to say good-bye. Little Ruth had a convulsion at 6 am and died. Frances remembers thinking that her family would never be happy again. Little Ruth was buried at Mount Carmel Baptist Church. At the time, Mella was 6 months pregnant with Edgeworth (Nookie).

Death of Little Ruth Hunt

News came to us Friday of the unexpecte[d] death of little Ruth, five-year old daughter o[f] Mr. and Mrs. Leigh Hunt, of the Mt. Carme[l] community. She died early Friday morning "Death loves a shining mark," and when th[e] death angel carried the soul of dear little Rut[h] away it bereft of one whom we loved. It pain ed those who loved her to give her up, but al[l] things work together for them that fear God We feel that the beautiful bud that has bee[n] plucked will bloom and be an ornament in th[e] flower gardens of Heaven. Burial took place a[t] Mt. Carmel, where the funeral was preache[d] Saturday morning at 11 o.clock by Rev. W. I[.] Coker. She is survived by her father and mothe[r] and the following sisters; Frances, Edn[a] Grace and Sara Bess, and one brother, Wesle[y] Hunt. We extend to them our sincerest sym pathy.

Chapter 11: Children and Descendants of Mella and Leigh Hunt — Sara Bess

Sara Bess Hunt (April 3, 1914 - July 5, 1980), like her sisters, received her BS degree in home economics from Winthrop College in Rock Hill where she was a member of Phi Kappa Phi, an honorary fraternity that encouraged superior scholarship. Later, she earned her Master's degree from University of Tennessee. She taught home economics on the high school and college levels (including Great Falls and Winthrop College) as well as being a supervisor of home economic programs in South Carolina. She was married to Edward Lloyd Galyon on December 21, 1944, in Easley. The couple lived in Knoxville, Tennessee all their married life.

Ed was president of Johnson and Galyon Construction Company, joining the organization in the 1940's. This well-respected firm has recently celebrated its 100th year. Ed was the estimator for the company, which built many landmarks in Knoxville and the surrounding area, including church

Sara Bess Hunt

buildings on the University of Tennessee campus.   Sara Bess served as a board member for the Red Cross. She was also a member of the APTA and the Dogwood Garden Club, as well as a Sunday school teacher and deacon in the Presbyterian Church. Whether involved in Boy Scouts, dissecting a cow's heart (bringing science to life in her classroom) or completing the finishing touches on a formal dress for Martha that she had designed and sewed, she strived to make so much possible for her children. She was a wonderful cook and gardener. The nieces remembered that a visit to her house included lunch and her pound cake as well as detailed information about her latest trip. Sara Bess had a kindness and the patience of Job, which was truly appreciated by all who knew her.

Ed died on August 14, 1968, and Sara Bess died twelve years later on July 5, 1980. Both are buried in Highland Memorial Cemetery in Knoxville, Tennessee.

Children of Ed and Sara Bess Galyon

Sara Bess and Ed had two children, Edward Lloyd and Martha Jane:

1. Edward Lloyd Galyon, Jr. (January 6, 1947) married Rebecca Jean Edwards (June 19, 1949). Edward and Rebecca have two children, one living:

    a. Edward Lloyd Galyon, III (September 15, 1980).

    b. Russell Wesley Hunt Galyon (July 26, 1985 -- March 5, 2007).

2. Martha Jane Galyon (November 25, 1954) married Robert Hester (February 23, 1953). Martha and Robert have two children:

    a. Virginia Elizabeth Hester (October 23, 1987) married William Trewhitt McGhee, IV (May 20, 1987) on April 8, 2015.

    i. William Trewhitt McGhee, V (July 19, 2020)

    b. Sara Rebecca Hester (July 19, 1985) married Christopher Allen Ivy (March 6, 1984) on December 1, 2018.

    i. Allen Robert Ivy (September 9, 2020)

Chapter 12: Children and Descendants of Mella and Leigh Hunt -- Edgeworth (Nookie)

Edgeworth Blythe Hunt (September 20, 1916—January 10, 1999) was always known as "Nookie", an affectionate name given to him by a household helper. He was named for his father's uncle, Colonel Edgeworth Blythe, a prominent attorney in Greenville. Nookie was the only Hunt child that never attended college. He spoke with a slight speech impediment, which was the result of a fever-induced convulsion that occurred when he was a

Edgeworth Blythe Hunt (Nookie)

baby. He married Margaret while he was living in Charleston, and they had a daughter Sandra, who died when she was 3 years old. The couple divorced.

Nookie then enlisted in the Navy and served in the Pacific during World War II. We were always excited when Nookie, looking so handsome in his sailor uniform, came to visit family while on leave.

Nookie later married Amelia. They had Barbara Leigh, and William Martin III. The couple divorced, and Nookie married Rachael, but this marriage also ended in divorce. Later, on May 1, 1980, Nookie married Irene, the real love of his life. They lived in Mobile, Alabama. In their later years they loved traveling around the country in a big motor

Nookie and his nieces and nephews

home. After Nookie's death, Irene lived the last part of her life in Bay Minette, Alabama.

There is a story about Nookie that Edna and Frances loved to tell: "One Saturday Nookie carried pigeons, baby rabbits, and bantam chicks to Mill Hill in Easley and traded them for a billy goat. He made a harness and cart and rode all around town, charging for goat rides." By the time he was 16 he had a paper route, a bicycle repair business. He was still young when he bought a Texaco station.

This entrepreneurial spirit never ceased. Nookie adored his mother and was devastated when she died. According to his wishes, he was buried beside his mother at Westview Cemetery in Easley.

Children of Edgeworth Hunt:

Nookie had three children.

1.   Sandra (1938-1941)

2.   Barbara Leigh Hunt (February 2, 1949)

3.   William Martin, III (July 20, 1950)

Chapter 13: Children and Descendants of Mella and Leigh Hunt — Bruce Hunt

Bruce Hunt

Bruce Oswald Hunt (January 22, 1919 - August 10, 1993) was named for Mella's brother. He was the youngest of Leigh and Mella's 7 children that would live to adulthood. He was

Bruce's and Katharne's wedding with Camella and Leigh Hunt

born on January 21, 1919, when the oldest, Frances, was 15. Frances and the younger girls delighted in his birth and treated him as their baby. Nookie was 4 years older and he and Bruce were best pals growing up. Like all the Hunt children, Bruce worked throughout his youth. Leigh owned a "hay, grain and provisions" store in downtown Easley and Bruce would tell of carrying 100 pound sacks of grain out to customers' waiting wagons and vehicles.

Nookie told the story that Bruce was notoriously frugal. After school, Nookie and Bruce would go to the soda fountain to get some refreshment. Nookie would order a Coca-Cola. Bruce would get water. He told Nookie, "If you are ever going be rich, you have to save your money."

Following in the footsteps of his brother Wesley, Bruce majored in accounting at the University of South Carolina. Since Wesley had been a charter member of Pi

Kappa Phi, Bruce joined that fraternity. He was active in the Intra Fraternity Council and a member of the German Club and Blue Key. He was a good student. After graduation, he joined J.W. Hunt and Company, a public accounting and auditing firm which his brother Wesley had purchased from Mr. William Rion upon retiring from the business.

In December, 1941, the Japanese attacked Pearl Harbor and the country went to war. Due to some physical problems, Bruce found it difficult to join the armed services. Wesley's friend, Frank Gary, a noted Columbia architect, was in charge of a significant area of the War Department in Washington and came to Bruce's aid and was able to help him get a Naval Commission. He was commissioned a Naval Officer and attended the Naval Supply Corps School at Harvard University in Boston. He graduated from there on December 4, 1942. After a brief visit to Easley and Columbia, he was sent to Treasure Island -- the Naval Depot in the San Francesco Bay -- to work as a supply officer. In May 1944, the supply ship *U.S.S. Shaula* (also known as 118) was commissioned and Bruce became a supply officer of that ship, which saw service in the Pacific.

Camella and Leigh with all seven of their grown children in 1948

During his war experience, Bruce always carried a pocket sized version of the Bible, which contained the Psalms, and he particularly found comfort in the 23rd Psalm. After the war, He visited war-torn Japan and China, including Nagasaki and Shanghai. He was discharged from the Navy on September 11, 1946 as a Lieutenant Commander.

Bruce returned to Columbia to rejoin J.W. Hunt and Company and to study to pass the CPA exam, which he passed with flying colors. Work at J. W. Hunt was hard, particularly because he was working for his brother. As preoccupied as he often was with the job, Bruce was occasionally absent minded.

This came into play when he had a blind date with Katharine Alice Otis (October 30, 1912—January 11, 2003), of Columbia. At the end of the date, they chatted in the parlor of Katharine's family's Pendleton Street home until late. After leaving, Bruce realized that he had forgotten his hat. Shy and embarrassed as he was, it took months before he contacted her again to get the hat. That second contact led to another date and, finally, marriage on Oct. 23, 1948.

Not long afterward, Bruce Hunt, Jr. was born on November, 2, 1949. Katharine Otis Hunt was born on May 29, 1952. Bruce and Katharine lived most of their married life in Columbia at 2740 Canterbury Road.

Bruce continued in the CPA practice throughout his life. He eventually became a partner in J.W. Hunt and Company and finally was Managing Partner after Wesley's retirement. During his life, he was President of the South Carolina Chapter of the American Association of CPA's. He was an active member of the First Baptist Church.

Throughout life, Bruce was a gentle, kind man and adored his family. He was very private but enjoyed his friends and Katharine's ability to entertain. He died on August 10, 1993, and is buried in Columbia at St. Peter's Catholic Cemetery, Elmwood. Katherine died on January 11, 2003 and is buried at his side.

Children of Bruce and Katherine Hunt

Bruce and Katherine Hunt had two children:

1. Bruce Oswald Hunt Jr (November 2, 1949) married Lynn Avery Wentworth (August 16, 1958), who is the mother of his two children. He later married Varian Crews Brandon (November 8, 1955).

   a. Marion Pendleton Hunt (October 9, 1987).

   b. Katharine Lynn Hunt (October 17, 1989).

2. Katharine Otis Hunt (May 29, 1952) married Steven Robert Baum (November 11, 1951). They have three children.

   a. Ellen Hunt Baum (November 21, 1977) married Michael Raymond Hollis (April 4, 1976).

   i. Hunt Michael Hollis (October 15, 2009).

b. Michael Benjamin Baum (January 14, 1981).

c. David William Baum (October 29, 1986).

Stillborn Infant

At age 39, on November 27, 1921, Mella gave birth to a stillborn infant daughter at home. Dr. Wyatt of Easley delivered the infant. Frances and Edna said she was a beautiful full-term baby. She is buried at Mr. Carmel Baptist Church. The baby was never named.

Chapter 16: Memories of Edna's Children

Judith White's Memories of Edna's Family's Journeys from Nashville to Easley

Every summer, my sister and I would be awakened about four in the morning by our mother, told to dress and, along with Daddy, we would pile into our 1941 Ford to start the eight-to-ten hour trip to our grandparent's home in Easley South, Carolina. The roads went across the Smoky Mountains and New Found Gap. We would always take along brown bags in case my sister got car sick, which happened frequently. We'd stop somewhere along the way and eat the warm, soggy sandwiches Edna had packed for our

The Easley house

lunch. Mother always drove for some reason -- probably because she thought she was a better driver. We had "440 air conditioning" in our car -- 4 windows down, 40 miles per hour. Upon arrival, our windblown hair looked like a family of rats had been nesting there for several weeks. Therefore, our mother, who always wanted look good for her sisters, would stop at a "filling station" outside of Easley. With her "beauty bag" in hand she'd hustle into the restroom, quickly remove her hair net, apply her makeup and change her rumpled dress. Then we would be ready to proudly make our grand entrance.

Suzanne, Linda and Judith

Every summer most of the family gathered at the Hunt house in Easley, an event eagerly anticipated by all. Mella prided herself in having plenty of everything for the entire family — linens, dishes and of course food. Ice cream freezers were cranked, beans snapped, butter churned, chickens' necks wrung, limas shelled, blackberries picked, and table extensions added for each family homecoming. The main meal was always in the middle of the day and preparations for it were begun immediately after a large breakfast.

After this wonderful daily feast, the enormous task of cleaning up would begin. The piles of dishes were washed and rinsed in two aluminum dishpans on the kitchen table. And someone was designated to carry out the delicious buckets of table scraps to "slop the hogs." During cleanup time some of the children would hide in the closet under the front hall steps to escape this chore, ignoring calls for help from their mothers and aunts. Later, the four sisters would retreat to the bedroom, cooled by the oscillating fan, lie on the beds in their slips, take a rest and chat.

Family gathered at Mella and Leigh's Easley home

In the late afternoons, with iced tea in hand, we would often gather on the front porch to rock and swing. Several times, Leigh, despite Mella's warnings, rocked off the porch, falling precariously into the bushes. A typical summer afternoon consisted of the cousins walking to the movie theater, followed by 5-cent ice cream at Frierson's Drug Store on the corner of Main and Pendleton. Evenings might bring Suzanne to the piano, along with the cousins, to sing hymns, Irish favorites, and hits of the day. This was something Mella loved! A trip to Easley was never complete without a visit to Ruth Hammond's Dress Shop, where Suzanne, Sarah and Linda would try on Ruth's latest fashions, with their mothers looking on. We would all feel so safe and happy in this house!

In the summer, when we were all gathered in Easley, Sunday afternoons were often a time when distance relatives and good friends would drop by to rock and visit on the front porch and, of course, admire Leigh and Mellas' growing grandchildren. The only compliment often issued to Edna's daughters, Suzanne and Judith, was, "Law, Edna, aren't they tall," a fact nobody denied, while the other granddaughters were described as "precious and angelic." Later, in the evening, when all the visitors had left, the sisters would discuss who had "fallen off" (lost weight), "fleshened up" (gained weight) or "broken" (aged) since the last visit.

Suzanne Potter's Memories of Edna's Family's Journeys from Nashville to Easley

Going to Easley was a huge occasion for my mother to have a chance to interact with her sisters, for she valued their approval and was always conscious of her relationship to them. Once we reached the house in Easley, we felt her relax in their company. My sister and I were so thrilled to be there -- it was the highlight of our childhood.

During every day of our visit, there was a huge midday meal. We called it "dinner", although that may seem strange to some people today. There would usually be around 10 to 12 adults and 10 to 12 children, mostly our cousins. I was annoyed at having to sit at the children's table (I was the oldest cousin). Edna and her three sisters would have gathered in the morning to divide out the preparation duties. Our mother was delegated to chop, wring the chickens' necks and singe the feathers by holding the bird over a newspaper torch. Meantime, the other sisters would be peeling potatoes; stringing green beans; making sweet tea; baking cornbread and blueberry or blackberry cobbler, and, with the older cousins' help, cranking the ice cream machine. After this huge meal, everyone took a nap.

Traveler on his "Stradivarius" fiddle

Chapter 17: Memories of Grace's Children

Memories of Sara Ferguson

Our dear Gram, Mella, was a wonderful cook; nothing gave her more pleasure than making something which her family enjoyed eating. When my brother Laurens was very young, about four or five, he liked to eat the icing off a cake, but not the cake itself. Having been warned by Mother that eating only the icing was bad manners, he subsequently declined a slice when we were visiting Mella in Easley. Nevertheless, insisting that he have some, she put before him a special slice of cake where she had removed the cake and back-filled the void with more icing. Laurens was amazed and delighted to have his all-icing cake.

Chapter 19: Memories of Sara Bess' Children

Memories of Martha Hester

Grace Fort

Great Falls holds such happy memories. Aunt Grace and Dr. Fort's wood-framed house was on a corner. The driveway wound around to the back and we would park at the back door. The slam of any screen door brings back a flood of memories. On her

Last photograph of all seven siblings gathering in 1973

back porch were always peaches or tomatoes laid out to ripen. When we walked into the kitchen, sitting on the stool was Grace's housekeeper Ella Mae. Her joyous grin and big hug were the best! Aunt Grace in her Tanner or Swirl dress would greet us. Pound cake and fresh peaches were the best!! Highlights of Great Falls included trips to Piggly Wiggly at FlopEye, driving through the town to look at the huge rocks in neighbors' yards, visiting Dr. Fort and Lauren's office, driving to the post office to check the box, driving Ella Mae home, or plinking the ivories on the upright piano that was in the dining room. Nothing was better than rocking on the front porch on the squeaky, rusty metal glider, and drinking iced tea or a Sundrop. Dr. Fort enjoyed his comfy chair in the living room, or being in the back room watching TV – Lawrence Welk (with cable TV, it was often available). Everyone loved Dr. Fort. He would drive through town and in the country in his beat up beige sedan with the back seat always full of stuff. As reported in the Great Falls paper in 1975, Dr Fort would throw candy out of the window to the children. The children would come to the edge of the road when they saw him coming. As a city girl, it was the craziest thing I'd ever seen.

Dr. Fort's Candy

For a generation, Dr. L.W. Fort has been tossing candy from his automobile to local youngsters and derived at least as much pleasure from it as the kids.

This week he announced that he's giving up the practice in the interest of the youngsters' safety. In view of the number of vehicles on our streets, we think the good Doctor has made a wise decision and we commend him for it.

Grace had come to Great Falls to teach. The teachers lived in a house/dormitory. (You could not teach if you were married) The story was told that Dr. Fort always found the best looking teacher in the fall at the beginning of the school year, and would court her throughout the year. Then there was the year that he found Grace Hunt. Fifteen years his junior she apparently melted his heart. He made her his bride in 1939 when she was 25 and he was 41.

Grace, like her sisters, was one smart woman! Along with raising a family, she was responsible for the rental houses that she and Dr. Fort owned – perhaps 60 or so. Of course she had hired men who worked on the houses, but Grace was responsible for the monthly rental collection. At the beginning of each month, when you heard the buzzer (which served as the doorbell) often someone had come to pay rent. They would come into the house and Grace would pull out the book, recording the transaction. In addition there was the wooden cabinet with cup hooks that held the keys to houses. It was quite the operation.

I never understood why it wasn't important to Aunt Grace, but for years the oven door was loose. When opened, one side would fall off of its hinge. I'm talking about a hot oven at 350 degrees, which required one to negotiate the door back in place.

I remember when Aunt Grace and Aunt Frances would argue about the making of gravy. After browning the flour in the grease one sister thought milk should be added to the hot skillet before adding water. The other thought the water should be added first. As a 10 year old, I didn't think it mattered. They had been making gravy in their own way for many years and both methods seemed to work quite well.

Aunt Grace's maid, Ella Mae

Ella Mae, Grace's maid, was such a wonderful woman. By the time I knew her, she had slowed down dramatically -- resting on a stool in the kitchen much of the time. But when you walked in the back door of Aunt Grace's house, you knew you

were loved. Ella Mae would envelop you in her voluminous bosoms and give you the sweetest hugs ever. Her voice was pure joy. She had the broadest smile and the whitest teeth. One gold tooth sparkled. Her skin was as black as could be imagined. She must have been at least 6 feet tall and very heavy. Honestly, I never remember Ella Mae without a smile.

I think someone brought Ella Mae to Grace's house in the mornings, but I often got to go along for the ride when it was time for her to go home. We would travel down the highway and then cut off on a dusty dirt road several miles from town. There was a community of small houses, somewhat adobe looking with lots of children playing out in the yards.

Brenda reminded me that Ella Mae had three children (and more than one of her grandchildren attended college, including Clemson). One morning Ella Mae didn't come in to work which was very unusual. Grace was concerned about her and called. As it turns out, Ella Mae had given birth to "a wee little baby" during the night, her pregnancy unbeknownst to anyone – including Ella Mae!

Judy said that Grace never got over the death of her dear friend Ella Mae.

Aunt Frances

As mother (Sara Bess) and I would travel from Great Falls to Charleston, we would often stop for lunch in Columbia at Katharine and Bruce's home. Their deeply wooded neighborhood was a welcomed respite from the noonday sun. Aunt Kat would greet us at the entrance of their split-level home. We would visit in the living room that opened onto their beautiful and manicured back yard and lawn, outlined with azaleas and tall trees. I always looked forward to seeing their big black dog, Pooh. Della would serve lunch as we were seated in

Edna, Frances, Sara Bess and Grace

the dining room. Aunt Kat's table was always set with china, crystal, and sterling. As road-weary travelers, we delighted in such pampering. After our delightful lunch and rest, we'd continue on our way to Charleston.

In the 1950's, Aunt Frances and Uncle Henry's house was on the Citadel campus in Charleston. The smells from the brackish waters lingered. Midday we would go upstairs, and rest or nap in our slips with the fan oscillating. Often, for dinner Uncle Henry would grill steaks – quite the treat. Before bedtime, he would put out orange juice in small glasses on the kitchen table to prepare for breakfast.

After Uncle Henry died, Aunt Frances moved to a beautiful guest house on King Street – South of Broad. Frances put slip covers over her furniture in the summer and then remove them in the fall to reveal her blue upholstery. Upstairs, the sisters would pair up in the two bedrooms and give each other facials and talk. Meals were always delicious. (Aunt Frances's yellow squash casserole is the most requested menu item at our house. I serve it at most dinner parties and picnics.)

Frances was always meticulously dressed. She wore lovely Lilly Pulitzer dresses or short sleeved white blouses with contrasting piping and skirts. She carried lovely fabric handbags. Frances would get together with girlfriends weekly to play bridge. They would meet mid-afternoon. Small sandwiches and gin and tonics accompanied the card games. At one point the ladies decided they were consuming too many calories – so they gave up the sandwiches. I just love that!

There was never a better place to walk than Charleston: beautiful homes with their private gardens, The Battery, and sweet little local shops were highlights. After an afternoon of seeing the sights of Charleston, we would return to the warmth and love found at Frances' home.

She nicknamed me "Motsie," a name that I'm now called by my friends' grandchildren.

Chapter 21: Memories of Frances' Children

Memories of Lisa Crowe

Blond Brownies

When my grandmother, Frances (I called her Mama) died, I got her recipe box. I don't think there's anything I could have inherited from her that would define her as strongly as those hand-written recipe cards. When we'd come to visit her in Charleston, South Carolina, we'd be served fried chicken, sweet iced tea made from Nestea mix, okra soup, Jiffy cornbread, fresh tomatoes and peaches from the downtown city market vendors, and fried shrimp – also purchased from the local vendors. I always loved the food she made and served at her house. I now realize that she must have carefully planned every meal before our arrival. She'd also plan visits to one or two local restaurants when we were in Charleston. We liked the Trawler and the Lorelei across the Cooper River, and Morrison's Cafeteria in town.

Frances and her sisters were always exchanging recipes. I remember when they were all making Dr. Bird cake – a cake with pineapple and nuts. They thought the name was so funny. And then there was the cake that had two jars of baby food plums in it, which was baked in a bundt pan. I remember my mother Linda talking with Frances and Grace about those cakes and making them. Frances didn't make desserts a lot, because she didn't want anyone to overeat and get F-A-T. We laugh about her preoccupation with overweight, but really, I am grateful that she and my mother didn't feed us too much sugar or bread, because I have not had to worry much about my weight during my life.

I remember Frances making Blond Brownies using a recipe given to her by her sister Grace. To me, the brown sugar and butter in them are a quintessentially Southern combination. When they were cool, she'd lift them out of the clear Pyrex pan with a thin wood handled spatula, which I still have, and serve them on an aqua-floral-bordered plate with a little handle on the side.

I miss my grandmother Frances so much still. Sometimes I will make something from her recipe box, or a dish from *Charleston Recipes*, and feel her close to me. There's something deeply touching about good food, lovingly prepared and served.

Blond Brownies: 1 cup flour; 1/2 tsp. baking powder; 1/8 tsp. soda; ½ tsp salt; sift these and set aside; then melt 1/3 cup margarine and add 1 cup brown sugar; cool; add 1 egg and 1 tsp. vanilla; add in sifted flour mixture and combine; spread onto greased baking sheet; sprinkle 1 pkg. chocolate chips on top; bake at 350 degrees for about 20 minutes.

Poppy Seed Dressing

I remember my mother Frances serving this dressing over fresh spinach with grapefruit sections for company. I never knew the recipe came from Aunt Sara Bess's daughter, Martha Hester until I pulled the recipe card out of the box recently. Mama loved Martha and all her nieces. She had a set of cork-backed placemats with birds on them that Martha had given her. Every time we'd use them, she'd remind me that they were a gift from Martha. I especially remember the placemat with a cardinal on it.

A day or two after Frances died, my mother Linda saw a cardinal out of her window at Dunbarton in Durham. Frances had always loved cardinals, and my mother had a strong sense that the cardinal was a message from Mama letting her know she was all right. I have read since then that many people believe cardinals are messengers from loved ones who have passed.

Poppy Seed Dressing: ¾ cup honey; 1 tsp salt; dash white pepper; 3/4 cup cider vinegar; 6 T. prepared mustard; 2 cups Wesson oil; 3-4 T. poppy seeds; 1 med. Onion, grated. Then mix.

Chapter 22: Closing Thoughts

Since July 10, 2002 marked the 100th wedding anniversary of Leigh and Camella Hunt, I had thought it appropriate that all Hunt descendants gather in Easley that summer, visit ancestral sites, remember our grandparents, and share among ourselves our memories in celebration of these special people. My cousins' childhood visits to Easley made an enormous impact on all of our lives.

The Departed since 2002

Sadly, since our gathering in Easley on July 10, 2002, several members of our family have passed away and I would like to remember them:

Linda Watkins (2002), Selina McNulty Hunt (2003), Katharine Otis Hunt (2003), Robert Bridger Hunt (2004), Martin Carmichael (2005), James Wesley Hunt III (2005), Hunt Galyon (2007), Chris Harlan (2008), Jack Lyle Ferguson (2008), Sara Catherine Jolley (2011), Laurens Fort (2017), Charles Ferguson (2017), and Ivan Haynes (2018), Sara Jefferies Ferguson (2018).

The Arkansas Traveler, as given by Leigh Hunt

What better way to close than by reflecting on Leigh's rendition of the Arkansas Traveler. The narrative and song follows:

About 40 years ago, when I was a young man, I was traveling through the mountainous part of the state of Arkansas. 'Twas a dark rainy day and I hadn't seen a house for several hours. My horse was powerfully tired. I came out into a clearing with a little log cabin in it. It had very little roof on it, and on the porch under a table sat an old man with a fiddle, playing this tune.

I said, "Hello, old man."

He said, "Hello yourself," and just kept right on playing.

"Old man, my horse is tired and hungry. We've been riding all day in this rain.

I wonder if we could spend the night with you."

"You can go to the Devil if you want to." He kept right on playing.

"Old man I want to board a week with you. "

"My little boy had gone to the mill and won't be back for a week."

"How far is it to Little Rock?"

"I don't know anything about a little rock, but there is a hell of a big one in my spring."

"Well, how far is it to Newport?"

"About 25 miles."

"Does the road fork between here and there?"

"I don't know anything about a fork, but it sure does split up powerfully."

"How can I cross that creek down there?"

"Ducks and geese generally swim it, and you can do the same."

"Why don't you cover your house, Sir?"

"Because it isn't raining."

"Why don't you cover it when it is not raining?"

"It is as dry as any man's house when it isn't raining."

There was a little field of corn over back of the house. It was yellow and only about as tall as this fiddle bow.

So I said, "Why don't you work that field of corn? It is mighty yellow and you won't make half a crop if you don't work it."

"I planted the yellow sort, and I planted it on the halves, and it is none of your business if I don't make any."

"Old man, why don't you play the turn to that tune?"

"There ain't no turn to it; it's just a straight tune."

"Bring me the fiddle, I'll play it for you."

The old man crawled out from under the table and handed me the fiddle and I played this song. "Light, stranger."

"Hitch your horse's head to the corncrib and his tail to the fodder stack, and come in this house. Kick the dog off that block and sit down and play the turn to that tune again."

"About 20 years ago I was in New Orleans and heard that tune. When I got home

I could play the first part of it.

"For 20 years I have been trying to play that last part.

"Stranger, play me the turn to that tune again."

"Son, go down to the bald faced popular where the speckled hen's nest used to be and get that bottle of whiskey out of that popular tree.

"Then go down in the hollow where we killed that buck this morning and cut some of the finest steaks for this gentleman to eat.

"And friend, play me that tune again."

A Memorable 1995 Visit to Explore Long-Ago Easley Memories

On Friday, on the last day in May, 23 years ago, in 1995, my sister, Suzanne and our cousin Linda Watkins Harland came to Charlotte to visit me. The next morning I announce, "We are going on a road trip." They did not know that I had arranged a visit to Easley, South Carolina and a stay in our grandparent's home, then owned by John and Christina Sitton. I had previously discussed the trip with the Sitton's and also with a cousin, B. L. Hendricks, who had promised to take us around the countryside and show us ancestral sites. Suzanne and Linda were greatly surprised and count the trip as a highlight in their memories of Easley and vacations with our Hunt grandparents. Soon after returning home, I wrote up a trip report. It is reproduced below, along with a thank-you note from Linda.

Our 1995 Trip to Easley

On Saturday morning, April 1, 1995, my sister Suzanne, our cousin Linda Watkins Harlan, and I left Charlotte, North Carolina for Easley, South Carolina. This was a long-dreamed-of trip back to our maternal grandparents' home. Leigh and Camella Hunt had moved to Easley in 1919 from their country home in Dacusville, South Carolina because of the closing of Mr. Carmel School. They would live in this wonderful two-story house at 301 South 1st Street until Camella's death in 1954. It was then sold to Ansel Jamison and his family. The Jamison family lived there until Ansel's death in 1994. It was then sold to John and Christina Sitton, a couple in their mid-thirties who have begun the difficult task of restoring the house. John Sitton's mother, Ruth Ragsdale, was a daughter of the Ragsdale's who lived next door to the Hunt's for many years.

The house had fallen into a poor state of repair, so obviously, we were very happy to know it was being restored by the loving hands of the Sitton's. There were some changes, but the house still has the wonderful feeling that we remembered as children. Our memories kept flooding back, and it was fun to think of times spent there with our precious grandparents. Some of the specific incidents were peeping over the bathroom transom at Aunt Sara Bess giving cousin Edward a bath, of smoking on the roof, of touching our toes on the ceiling while swinging on the porch swing. Our grandmother's loving, sunny disposition and the wonderful smells coming out of her simple little kitchen made us realize the reason we looked forward to our visits there.

Christina and John had invited us to spend the week-end, which made our visit even more special. We arrived around noon. After a quick tour of the house and barn and the Wyatt house across the street, which has also been recently renovated, we had lunch with Christina and John. After lunch, we walked to the Westview cemetery where our grandparents and Henry Watkins (Linda's father) are buried. Linda's mother, Frances Hunt Watkins will also be there beside her husband and her parents.

Suzanne announced after returning from our walking trip that an excursion to the Swirl Outlet (leisure-like housecoats) was a must. We all drove to Swirl where Suzanne replaced her old one. She had been wearing a ragged navy blue one with the pockets falling off, which, for many years, had belonged to our mother, and had been purchased long ago at the same store.

When we returned to the house, John Sutton's mother, Ruth Ragsdale, and our Mother's first cousin, B. L. Hendricks, were waiting. B. L. drove us up to Griffin Church and environs, about 10 miles from Easley, near Pickens. Griffin Church was built with money from a land grant given by our great-great-great-grandfather, Sargent Griffin, and his wife, Averilla, in 1857. They were a wealthy farm family in the Glassy Mountain area. The original deed, which is at the church, is in his handwriting. One of his daughters, Averilla Griffin, who married H. J. Anthony, were charter members. They are our great-great-grandparents and parents of "Betty" Vashtie Elizabeth Anthony, who married David Erwin Hendricks, our great-grandparents. David Ervin owned a post office, cotton gin, and general store, and our grandmother Camella was their child. David Ervin was also a stockholder in the first cotton mill in the area.

After we left Griffin Church, we went to Betty and Ervin Hendricks's house. No one was living there, so we were able to browse through the house where our grandmother Camella grew up. Our mother and her siblings visited there frequently, also. In the old Glassy Mountain cemetery above the house, David Ervin's parents,

George and Louvicy Mullinax Hendricks are buried. George Hendricks burned to death while clearing fields in 1881.

Leaving this area, we went a few miles to the old house where George and Louvicy (David Hendricks's parents) lived. It was now occupied by an "old drunk" named Claude and his girlfriend. B. L. Hendricks said he had been told that Sherman came through and threatened to burn the house down if they didn't give up their horses. When the men pulled hot coals out of the fireplace and onto the floor, the horses were quickly handed over! Behind the house is an enormous oak tree, reported to be one of the largest in the state. George Hendricks was a teacher, farmer and shoemaker. Two of their sons, Baylus and William Fields, were killed in the Civil War.

Ervin, our great-grandfather was the only surviving son, so he received the family land. Ervin owned thousands of acres, including the three mountains behind their home.

Next, we went to the deteriorated home of our Grandmother's oldest brother, Ed (1870-1951) who is also buried at Griffin Church, where he served as a deacon and church clerk. Ed Hendricks had nine children and was married to Eliza Jane Brown.

Returning to Easley, Christina had dinner waiting. Afterward, we walked up the street to visit ninety-one-year-old Aileen Wyatt, who was a friend of our mother and grandmother. "Miss Aileen" had taught in the Easley High School and lived with her maiden sister Ethyl, throughout their professional life in a little house next to her parents' home.

That evening we just had such a wonderful time, surrounded by the memories of our mothers and grandmother. We truly felt our Gram's spirit. We slept in bedrooms upstairs that we had slept in as children. But before, leaving we signed the door to the closet under the steps that led upstairs, a space that had been a favorite "hiding place" when visiting as children.

Sunday morning after a brief walk around the area, we ate breakfast at Shoney's. Then back to Charlotte. What an unforgettable week-end, and made very special by the three of us being together and sharing these wonderful childhood memories.

P.S.: A sad note to this great trip was a call two weeks later from John Sitton, who informed us of the death of B.L. Hendricks. He was such a dear man and we will treasure the memory of our brief meeting.

Linda's Thank You Note

Linda's April 7, 1995 thank-you note to me follows:

Dearest Judy,

Didn't we have a wonderful time at Gram's house and being together!! I wouldn't take anything for that trip and appreciate so much your arranging everything and sharing all the old memories with us.   "No spot is so dear to my childhood."   The old barn is exactly as I remembered it and, even though Gram's house isn't exactly the same now, the essentials are the same – those doors, door knobs and the bead and board ceilings and the front porch. It was our childhood and our Gram and Leigh revisited. It was wonderful. Please go back with me one day -- we really did go home again.   I remembered why that closet was in the upstairs bathroom -- the teachers would go home for the summer and would store their things in there so we could have room when we came. Definitely, the love seat you have was by the steps.

Appendix

IN MEMORIAM

Mrs. Betty Anthony Hendricks

Mrs. Betty Anthony Hendricks was born in the Griffin section of Pickens county in the year 1849 and was the daughter of Henry Jacob Anthony and Averilla Griffin Anthony. She was married to David Ervin Hendrickks in the year 1867, age 20 years, and was the mother of the following children: W. E. Hendricks, J. W. Hendricks, G. R. Hendricks, D. F. Hendricks, all of Pickens county; Mrs. Leigh Hunt, Easley; Mrs. J. F. Williams, Sumter; J. H. Hendricks, Pickens; B. L. Hendricks, Dacusville; Mrs. J. H. G. McDaniel, Pickens; P. O. Hendricks, Pickens; Miss Nora Hendricks, who died when quite a young woman, and Mrs. Lula Cox, who died several years ago.

It is said that "A life is the product of the incarnated personalities of generations of forbearers," and so to Mrs. Betty Anthony Hendricks. From her godly, pioneering ancestry came with her qualifications, courage born of conviction, steadfastness of purpose, unwavering faith, self-sacrificing devotion for everything that was good, and above all she possessed a vision which is more than the faculty of sight. She was a woman in her day that looked out for her church, family and community as well as far beyond the day's realities to the splendid possibilities of tomorrow.

Though active along many useful lines in her community and day, her church (Griffin, named and established by her family) as long as she was able, always came first. Nothing was ever permitted to crowd out its claim upon her time and effort. No one ever went to her church that wasn't welcome to her home and hospitality. She has been known for years to have with her after service for dinner from twenty-five to thirty persons to partake of a meal she fixed with her own hands. Her pastors were welcomed on all occasions to her home and she was never absent from a Saturday or Sunday service unless providentially hindered. She made large controbutions of money and time to Old Griffin and helped build the new church. She was of that humble type that desired that her kindness to others be known only to herself. As the writer of this sketch, I knew her when she was very active but do not know myself, nor have ever talked with anyone that had ever seen "Miss Betty," as everyone called her, enter her own church from the back. She always came in the side entrance and slipped gently into her place, with a worshipful air at all times. Space would not permit to tell all of her efficient work in the church and among the folks in her community. Her life was conformed to teachings of God's word and not to the custom of the day. She was conscientiously strict in her discipline of self and that example she set for her family and those that her life came in contact with. She was ever lenient in her judgment of others and her justice was always tempered with tenderness of mercy. Her home was a constant enter of business interests and dealings with one's fellowmen, but whatever they might be "Miss Betty" saw to it that everyone was happy when the settlement was made.

The interest of others welfare always took precedence over all else. It was never said of her that she had a trace of narrowness or bigotry. She loved all alike. This was true in her relation to her family, friends and community. No mother ever worked harder or with more singleness of purpose. I quote from her friends: "Miss Betty was the best woman I ever saw or knew. She weighed all things and dealt accordingly. She had words of consolation for all, others looked to her in distress. As long as she could she was of that bright, happy disposition and all that knew her loved her."

The following well known words seem eminently appropriate to this splendid life of lengthened days, which was written by Clyde Edwin Tuck:

Why should we for the sainted dead
    repine,
Friends who no longer journey with
    us here?
Though here no more their happy
    faces shine,
We feel, at times, they may be very
    near.

They wait ahead and are not lost
    we know,
Except to mortal sense—somehow,
    somewhere,
They live and love again, while here
    below
We glimpses catch of their celestial
    sphere.

For love can never change in influence,
It reaches out from Heaven to
    earth,
All suffering and care to recompense,
And to the darkened soul brings new
    birth.

Love that rejoices in another's
    good,
Like that our friends departed for
    us bore,
And meekly all the darts of pain
    withstood,
Can perish not, but lives for evermore.

It still enfolds us, and would light
    our way,
Would act as anchor to our faith and
    hope,
It bids us doubt not, but watch and
    pray,
Until truth's dawn breaks in life's
    higher light.

Mrs. Hendricks Taken By Death

Mrs. Betty Hendrix, 83, died at the home of her daughter Friday morning at 10 o'clock. She had been an invalid for a number of years, but her more recent illness was of only a few days.

Mrs. Hendricks, a member of one of the county's most prominent families, was a daugtter of the late Jacob Anthony and Avarilla Griffin Anthony. She was a widow of the late D. Ervin Hendricks, and for the past 18 months has been living with her daughter, Mrs. J. H. G. McDaniel, near here. Previous to that she had resided at her home near Griffin church.

Surviving are three daughters, Mrs. Leigh Hunt, Easley; Mrs. J. F. Williams, Sumter; Mrs. J. H. G. McDaniel, Pickens; seven sons, Ed Hendricks, J. W. Hendricks, G. R. Hendricks, D. F. Hendricks, J. H. Hendricks, P. O. Hendricks, all of Pickens; one sister, Mrs. Sallie Freeman, Pickens. In addition there are 65 grandchildren.

Funeral services will be held from the Griffin Baptist church at 11 o'clock Sunday morning. Officiating will be the Rev. A. E. Howard, the Rev. F. S. Childress and the Rev. T. B. Lanham. Interment will be made in the family plot in the church cemetery.

Active pallbearers will be grandsons of the deceased, Jim Edd Hendricks, D. I. Hendricks, Robert Hendricks, Jr., George Cox, Wesley Hunt and John Frank Williams, Jr.

Composing the honorary escort will be G. E. Cureton, W. E. Finley, George Brezeale, J. R. Connely, J. D. Holder, Sr., Dr. J. L. Valley, Dr. R. A. Kirksey, T. T. Hallum, O. T. Hinton, E. F. Alexander, R. E. Lewis, B. C. Ligon, W. R. Cantrell, E. L. Jones, B. T. McDaniel, A. C. Smith, G. H. Hendricks, A. J. Boggs, Sr., S. H. Brown, J. F. Childs, S. L. Pace, S. B. Dorr, H. D. Leslie, J. M. Hayes, J. A. Robinson, Easley; Ernest Folger, T. L. Bivens, Frank McFall, B. Lewis, John B. Craig, B. H. Powers, T. T. Hughes and John Roper, Greenville.

LEIGH HUNT

Funeral services for Leigh Hunt, 93, were to be conducted Wednesday at 3 p.m. at the Robinson Funeral Home by Dr. Norman R. Lewis, with burial following in West View Cemetery.

Mr. Hunt, formerly of Easley, died at 2:40 a.m. Tuesday in a Columbia rest home after an extended illness.

A native of the Mt. Carmel section of Pickens County, he was a son of the late William and Martha Blythe Hunt. In 1919 he moved to Easley where he was a merchant and farmer. Since the death of his wife, Mrs. Camella Hendricks Hunt, in 1954, he had lived in Tennessee and for the past two weeks in Columbia. He was a member of the Easley First Baptist Church.

Surviving are three sons, J. Wesley Hunt and Bruce Hunt, both of Columbia, and E. B. (Nookie) Hunt of Mobile, Ala.; four daughters, Mrs. Frances Watkins of Charleston, Mrs. Edna Willis of Nashville, Tenn., Mrs. Grace Fort of Fort Mill and Mrs. Sara Bess Gallyon of Knoxville, Tenn.

Pallbearers were B. L. Hendricks, Smith E. Hendricks, Jack Ragsdale, Sam Williams, Craig Williams, James H. Hendricks, Jr., Jim Ed Hendricks and Lehman Bauknight.

MRS. LEIGH (Camella Hendricks) HUNT

We, the members of the T. E. L. Class of the First Baptist Church, Easley, S. C., wish to pay tribute to a loved and devoted member, Mrs. Camella Hendricks Hunt, whose passing, on April 23, 1954, has saddened our hearts and caused us to feel a deep sense of personal loss.

She was a devoted wife, a loving mother, and a true friend to her neighbors as she tried to practice the life described in Proverbs 31. Her Christian character and cheerful disposition were an inspiration to all who knew her. We thank God for her life in our midst and her influence for good. Surviving are her husband, Leigh Hunt; four daughters, Mrs. Edna Willis, Nashville, Tenn., Mrs. Frances Watkins, Charleston; Mrs. Grace Fort, Great Falls, and Mrs. Sara Bess Galyon, Knoxville, Tenn; three sons, J. Wesley and Bruce, both of Columbia, S. C., and E. B. (Nookie), Chattanooga, Tenn.; sixteen grandchildren; three brothers, Ossie, Frank, and Jim Hendricks, all of Pickens; and two sisters, Mrs. J. H. G. McDaniel, Pickens, and Mrs. J. Frank Williams, Sumter.

We express to her family our sincere love and heartfelt sympathy and ask that a copy of this memorial to her be sent to them, a copy recorded in the minute book of the T. E. L. Class, and a copy sent to The Baptist Courier for publication.— Committee: Mrs. J. R. Wyatt, Mrs. Bowen Stewart, Mrs. G. B. Hamilton

July 14. 1881

HORRIBLE DEATH.—Mr. George Hendricks, aged 74 years, met with a horrible death on last Thursday evening. It appears that he had gone out for the purpose of burning off a turnip patch, but how he came to be burned to death no one knows. It is supposed, however, that he had probably been overcome by heat, or had taken a swimming in the head, which he was at times subject to, and had fallen down, and before he could recover the fire had burned to him and done its deadly work. He had fallen with his head near a fence, and seems to have been on the side opposite the fire, but the fence caught and the rails burned in two and fell across him. Dr. Earle says that in the fall he may have struck his head against the fence, and the jar may have made him insensible. His hat was found near him burning, and a key to a chest, in which he kept his land papers and what money he kept about him, which he carried fastened to a button on the waistband of his pants, was found still on him, and there was no evidence whatever of foul play. Dr. Earle informs us that the body was so terribly burned the limbs would almost fall from the body from a slight touch, and that the face and front of the skull were burned until they would crumble by a touch. The abdomen was burned until the intestines fell out. Those who saw the remains say it made the heart sick to look upon them. Mr. Hendricks was a member of the Methodist Church and was one of our most honorable and respectable citizens.— He leaves a widow and several children, besides other relatives to mourn his death, to whom we extend our heartfelt sympathies.

① July 23, 1802
② July 6, 1881

Leigh Hunt Family Leaves Easley After 36 Years

By CHARLES KING, JR.

After 36 years in Easley the Leigh Hunt family returned to their home on South First St. for the last time on a recent week-end. Mr. Hunt and six of his seven children gathered for a final reunion in the big white house which he and Mrs. Hunt built in 1919 when they first moved to Easley from their country home near Dacusville.

Over the years that house has come to symbolize for the people of Easley the achievements and contributions of one of the city's leading families.

Since Mrs. Hunt's death last year Mr. Hunt, now 87, has spent most of his time away from Easley visiting in the homes of his children. The family recently decided that it would be best to sell the home and divide the household belongings, and last week final transactions were completed.

Mr. and Mrs. Ansel Jameson and their four young daughters will be the new owners and occupants of the Hunt home.

One of the Hunt daughters had said that perhaps they shouldn't sell the house because it would be wonderful to have it here to come back to from time to time. But Mr. Hunt felt otherwise. "Your mother and I put up this dwelling for a big family, and it's only right that a big family should always live here."

He was highly pleased at the thought of the four Jameson daughters growing up in his home; four daughters were among the seven Hunt children reared there in days gone by.

Mr. and Mrs. Hunt had always lived in Pickens and Greenville Counties. She was Camella Hendricks of Pickens before her marriage on July 10, 1902, and he came from pioneer families in Greenville County. The Hunts celebrated their golden wedding anniversary two years before Mrs. Hunt died on April 23, 1954.

The couple always kept up with happenings in Easley, and unlike many elderly persons, took an active part in the civic life of the community. Mrs. Hunt's last neighborhood project was an Easter egg hunt, given for children on the street only a few days before her death.

She always kept apples and candy ready for the youngsters who called—one little fellow used to make a dash for the refrigerator the moment he entered the house; he knew where Mrs. Hunt kept the goodies. The trick-or-treat callers of Halloween were never forced to resort to tricks at the Hunt home.

The sound of childish voices was seldom stilled for any great length of time in the big white house. Soon after the Hunt children departed, the Hunt grandchildren began arriving for prolonged visits, and in between there were always the students passing to and from Easley High School less than a block away.

Some of Easley's best known teachers—Miss Eva VanLandingham, principal of West End School; Miss Alma VanLandingham, principal of Arial School; and Miss Helen Mozingo of the high school faculty—lived for years in the Hunts' upstairs apartment, so that almost no school activity passed without the couple's noting it.

Mr. and Mrs. Hunt took great pleasure in sitting on their spacious front porch, which a more leisurely age would have called a piazza, and speaking to the school children as they passed on the street.

The seven children have all been successful in later life, or have married husbands with impressive records.

Frances, the eldest daughter, is now Mrs. J. H. Watkins of Charleston, where Colonel Watkins is professor of geology and biology at The Citadel. Edna, Mrs. L. J. Willis, lives in Nashville, Tenn.; her husband, Dr. Willis, is supervisor of the Nashville elementary schools.

Many Easley residents will remember the Willis daughter, Suzanne, a talented violinist who played often for local church services. Now Mrs. William P. Parker, Jr., she continues to serve with the Nashville Symphony Orchestra while her husband completes his senior year at Vanderbilt Medical School.

Grace Hunt Fort, the third daughter, married Dr. L. W. Fort, a dentist in Great Falls.

Sara Bess, the youngest daughter, is Mrs. E. L. Galyon of Knoxville, Tenn., where her husband operates a construction company. She is the mother of the youngest of the 17 Hunt grandchildren, six-month-old Martha. Mr. Hunt was especially pleased to see his latest grandchild christened this Easter, for she bears a name which has become a family tradition—Mr. Hunt's mother, grandmother and great-grandmother were all named "Martha."

The eldest son, J. Wesley, C. P. A., is president of J. W. Hunt and Co., an accounting firm in Columbia. His son, Jimmy, the oldest grandchild, will be a senior at the University of South Carolina this fall.

"Nookie" Hunt (his name is E. B., but his sisters said, "If you don't say Nookie no one in Easley will know who you're talking about.") lives in Chattanooga, Tenn., where he owns a chain of drive-in restaurants.

Bruce, the Hunt's youngest, is also a C.P.A. and a member of his brother's firm in Columbia.

All the children, with the exception of "Nookie," came back last week-end. Mr. Hunt is stopping by Chattanooga for a visit with the one absentee on his way for an extended visit at his daughter's home in Nashville.

Mrs. Hunt always prided herself on having enough of everything—bedding, china, etc.—for all the family to visit at one time. When the sons and daughters began breaking up the household, they discovered that it was a momentous job—"The accumulation of 50 years," Mrs. Fort said.

As Mr. Hunt moves from home to home—winters in South Carolina and summers in Tennessee—he will find something to remind him of the big white house in Easley at each and every place.

All the family say that they will always call Easley home. Each subscribes to The Progress and join with Mr. Hunt in following the activities of the town. Like their father they declare, "We're coming back to Easley."

The Hunts were members of the First Baptist Church, where Mr. Hunt served for many years as a deacon. He has seen his church and his city grow phenomenally in the 36 years since he built his home on what was then Church Street, but in a more systematized age has received the somewhat deflating title, "South First St."

Church St. in the early Hunt days was not much more than a dirt path running down into a swamp. "We felt as though we were in the country," said Mrs. Watkins. The path is now a boulevard with curb, gutter and sidewalk; the swamp is now Easley High School's Brice Field.

The Hunt family and the town have grown together, and it can probably be truly said that Easley is the better for having known the Hunts. The city will not soon forget the untiring couple and their energetic family who made a landmark of the friendly white house on "Church St."

69

LEIGH HUNT & CO.

"THE HAPPY FEED STORE"

WHOLESALE & RETAIL

HAY, GRAIN AND PROVISIONS

PHONE 195

EASLEY, S. C.————————————*192*

SOLD TO _Jack_

What the stocking said
All day we carry toes;
Tonight we carry candy.
Christmas comes but once a year
And then we are so handy

Boots and little tired shoes
We kick 'em off in glee
It is fun to hang up here
And Santa Claus to see.

Christmas morning down we come;
The sweet things tumble out,
And then we carry toes again,
And have to trot about

Mr., Mrs. Leigh Hunt Have Golden Anniversary Party

EASLEY—Mr. and Mrs. Leigh Hunt were honored on their golden wedding anniversary recently when their children entertained for them at an informal reception at the Hunt residence between the hours of 4:30 and 6 p. m.

Receiving with Mr. and Mrs. Hunt were all of their children: Mrs. J. H. Watkins of the Citadel, Mr. and Mrs. L. J. Willis of Nashville, Tenn., Mrs. L. W. Fort of Great Falls; Mr. and Mrs. E. L. Galyon of Knoxville, Tenn., J. W. Hunt of Columbia, Edgeworth Hunt of Charleston, and Mr. and Mrs. Bruce Hunt of Columbia.

Arrangements of yellow gladioli, carnations and chrysanthemums were placed in the reception hall, living room and dining room. Mrs. Hunt's corsage was a white orchid with yellow throat and Mr. Hunt wore a yellow boutonniere.

A musical program was presented throughout the afternoon by Mrs. J. L. Camp, vocalist, Mrs. James Stuckey, pianist, and Miss Suzanne Willis of Nashville, Tenn., violinist, a granddaughter.

Refreshments consisting of ham biscuits, assorted cakes, nuts, mints and punch were served in the dining room by Misses Sara Fort of Great Falls, Linda Watkins of Charleston, Judith Willis of Nashville, Tenn., and Marie Hunt of Columbia, granddaughters of the honored couple.

Others assisting in entertaining the guests were Mrs. W. H. Ragsdale, Misses Aleen and Ethel Wyatt, Mrs. Reuben Sitton, Mrs. George Hamilton, Mrs. Lehman Bauknight, Mrs. Jones Lanford, and Mrs. Francis Alward of Pickens.

Additional grandchildren present were Jim, Will, Leigh and Bob Hunt of Columbia, Laurens Fort of Great Falls, Edward Galyon of Knoxville, Bruce Hunt Jr., of Columbia, and Barbara Hunt of Charleston.

Out-of-town relatives attending included the following brothers and sisters of Mrs. Hunt: Mrs. J. Frank Williams of Sumter, Mrs. J. H. G. McDaniel and Frank, J. H. and P. O. Hendricks of Pickens.

Mrs. Hunt is the former Camella Hendricks of Pickens, the daughter of the late Betty and Irvin Hendricks, and Mr. Hunt's parents were Martha Blythe and William U. Hunt of Greenville.

Ancestors of Cora Camella Hendricks going back to late 1700s

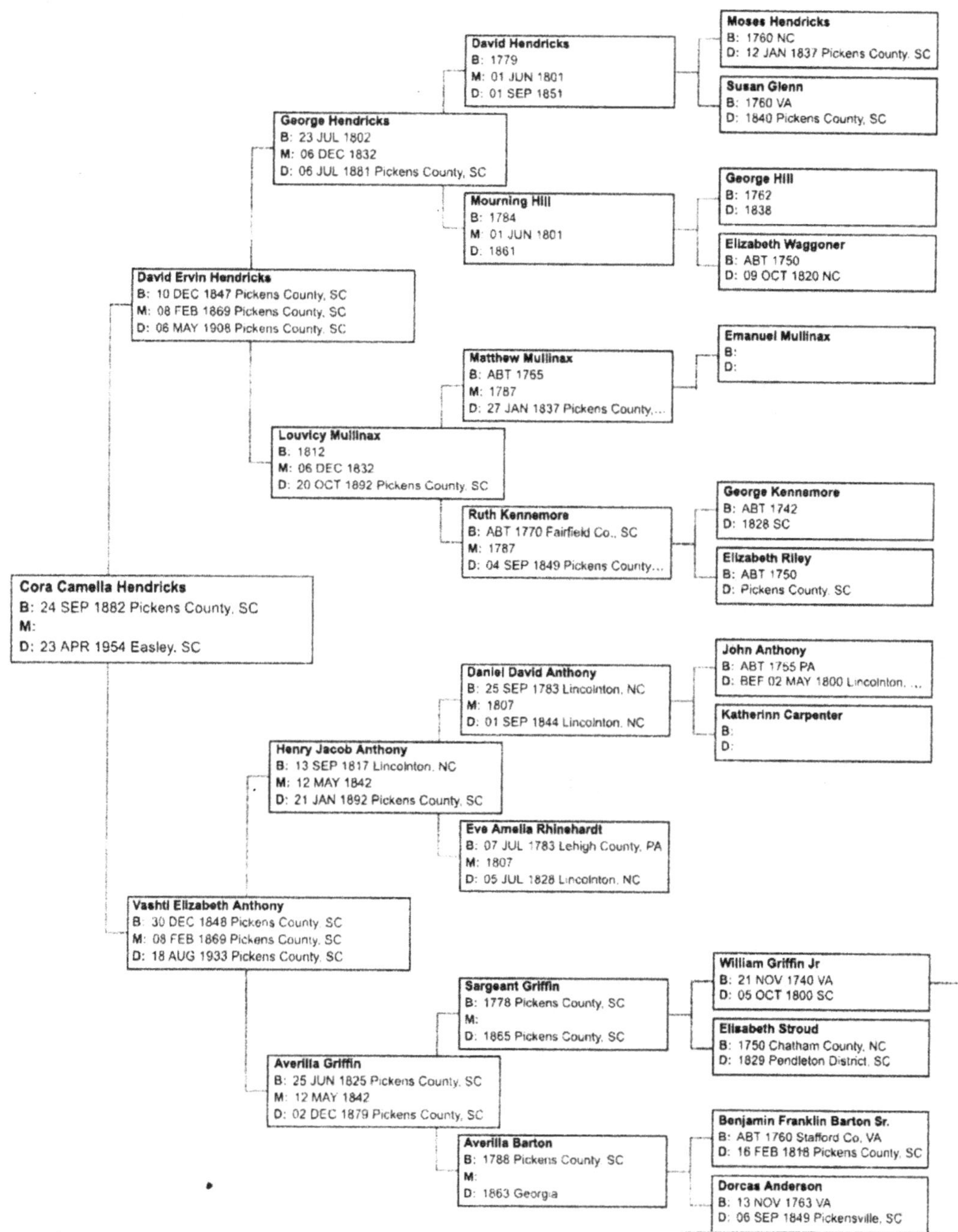

Ancestors of Leigh Hunt going back to late 1700s

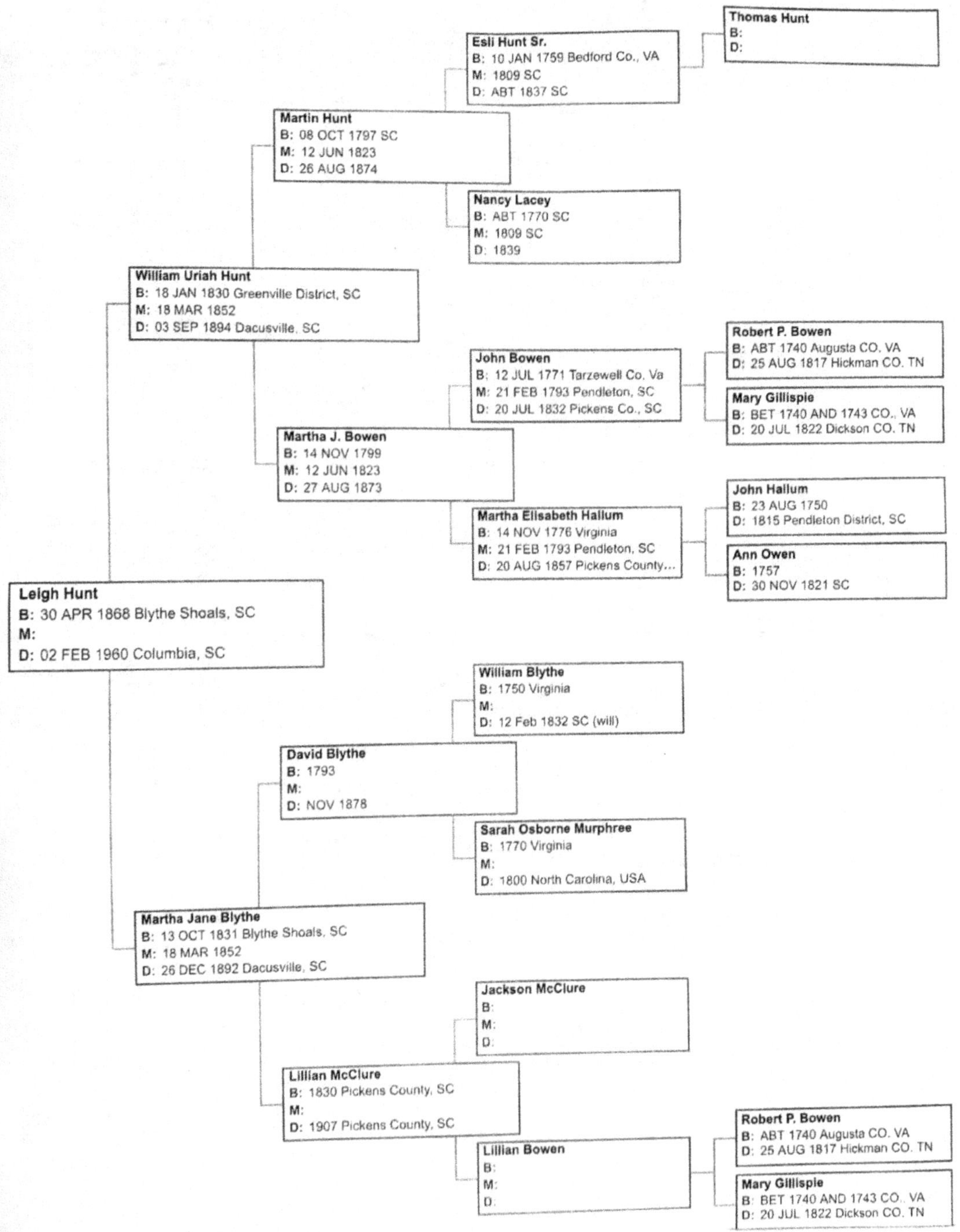

www.ingramcontent.com/pod-product-compliance
Lightning Source LLC
Chambersburg PA
CBHW080002180726
48002CB00020B/2922